Delicious Cont‹

CW00347376

Sally

My love of baking started in Hayes, Middlesex, in the 1970s, when I learned to bake cakes with my Mum, kneeling up on a kitchen stool to reach the worktop and licking the bowl and spoon! Following marriage to Keith (whose favourite is Bakewell Tart), two wonderful children, Chris (Choc Chip Banana Cake) and Vicky (Carrot Cake), and a move to Northwood, I continued to bake: birthday and Christmas cakes for friends and family, bakes for school and church fundraisers, cakes for the church coffee shop. Keith regularly came home from work to find a kitchen full of cake!

In August 2014, following Keith's early retirement and with Chris and Vicky grown up, we moved to Keswick in the beautiful Lake District. Keith and I took over ownership of Glencoe Guest House on Helvellyn Street. We decided from the start that I would bake a cake each day for our guests to enjoy after a long day in the hills, cycling around the Lakes, or simply enjoying all that Keswick has to offer by way of retail therapy, cinema, theatre and lake views.

As keen walkers ourselves Keith and I decided that Keswick Mountain Rescue was the perfect charity to receive the donations left by our guests in exchange for a slice of homemade cake. Between August 2014 and Summer 2019 Glencoe Guest House so far has raised over £2500 for KMR in donations from our wonderful guests.

Over the years guests and other friends have often asked for my recipes. I hope that Bakes from the Lakes will enable you to bake some delicious treats for your family and friends – and raise more much needed funding for the vital work of Keswick Mountain Rescue.

I have always loved eating the cakes as much as baking them, and I hope you will too.

Sally's Guide to Great Bakes

 Always preheat the oven to the temperature required. Some ovens vary and fan ovens can operate at lower temperatures.

 Prepare the cake tins before starting on the cake. Baking parchment is great, as are the cake tin liners and pre-cut circles for the sandwich tins that you can buy at a variety of outlets.

 Check you have all the ingredients before you start baking. Nothing worse than getting halfway through and finding out a trip to the supermarket is required!

 Soften the butter/margarine and sugar in the microwave to save on elbow grease.

 Use a cake skewer to check the cakes are thoroughly cooked. Insert at a 45° angle and leave for 10 seconds before removing. If it comes out clean the cake is ready to come out of the oven. If it is sticky put the cake back and bake for a few more minutes, closing the oven door carefully to prevent the cake from sinking.

 Leave the cake in the tin for about 10 mins before turning out onto a cooling rack to cool completely.

 When whisking egg whites, ensure the bowl is clean and dry to get the best results.

Using a spatula to scrape out the bowl will ensure no ingredients are wasted, however, licking the bowl and the spoon once the cake mix is in the tin is one of the perks of happy baking so enjoy and don't feel embarrassed!

 A spare cake tin liner or some parchment paper, placed over the cake mixture before putting it in the oven will prevent the cake from overbrowning while cooking.

 Having a good radio station or favourite CD on in the back ground adds to a happy baking atmosphere. Who doesn't love a little dance in the kitchen whilst whisking and stirring?

 A spoonful of Love adds that last little special something into every cake made at Glencoe Guest House. Just blow a kiss over the cake as it goes in the oven and "Voila" everyone will be in love with your cakes.

Gluten-free (GF) friendly recipes

Sticky Stem Ginger Cake - Pg 10
Replace 225g self raising flour with 170g GF s/r flour and 55g ground almonds

Moist Fruit Cake - Pg 17
Replace 225g self raising flour with 170g GF s/r flour and 55g ground almonds

Carrot and Almond Cake - Pg 25
Rreplace 75g self raising flour with 75g GF s/r flour

Banana Choc Chip Cake - Pg 29
Replace 285g self raising flour with 225g GF s/r flour and 60g ground almonds

Blueberry & Almond Cake - Pg 34
Replace 125g self raising flour with 125g GF s/r flour

Whole Orange Cake - Pg 37
Replace 85g self raising flour with 85g GF s/r flour

Victoria Sponge - Pg 42
Replace 225g self raising flour with 170g GF s/r flour and 55g ground almonds

Pineapple Upside Down Sponge - Pg 46
Replace 225g self raising flour with 170g GF s/r flour and 55g ground almonds

The Icing on the Cake

Butter Icing

Ingredients: 140g butter, softened. 280g icing sugar, sifted.
1-2 tbsp milk. 1tsp vanilla extract.

Method: In a large bowl, soften the butter in the microwave until
soft. Add the icing sugar and beat until smooth. Gradually add
the milk and vanilla extract and beat the mixture until creamy
and smooth. You may not need all the milk!

Water Icing

Ingredients: 125g icing sugar, sifted. 15ml warm water.

Method: Put the sifted icing sugar into a small or medium
bowl and gradually add the water. Mix together until the icing
becomes thick enough to coat with a back of a spoon. If
necessary, add more water (a drop at a time) until it is thick/
thin enough to use.

Chocolate Frosting

Ingredients: 50g butter. 1 tbsp milk.1 tbsp golden syrup.
15g cocoa. 175g icing sugar

Method: Put the butter, milk and syrup in a bowl and gently
melt in the microwave ensuring it doesn't get too hot! Stir it
all together until the mixture has blended then sift in the icing
sugar and cocoa until the icing comes away from the sides of
the bowl.

Fruit Scones

Ingredients

115g butter
115g caster sugar
454g self raising flour
235ml milk
170g sultanas

baking tray

cooking time:
15-20mins @ 220°c

Method

In a blender mix the flour, sugar and butter until finely blended and no trace of butter. Transfer to a mixing bowl and add the sultanas and stir to evenly distribute them before adding the milk. Stir well until the ingredients are all combined then leave for approximately 10mins.

Dust the work surface with some flour and tip out the mixture then gently pat down to approximately 1" (2.5cm) thick. Using a 2" (5cm) round cutter, cut out the scones and place on a lined baking tray. Makes 10 – 12 large scones. Brush with milk or a beaten egg before putting in the oven.

Cheese Scones

Replace the sultanas with the same amount of grated cheddar cheese for yummy cheese scones, adding chopped olives, chilli flakes, ground pepper, chopped sundried tomatoes, walnuts..... whatever takes your fancy. Be creative, have fun, and enjoy testing the new flavours.

Sticky Stem Ginger Cake

Ingredients

115g butter
115g dark brown sugar
225g self raising flour
1 egg
2-3 tbsp ground ginger
1 tsp cinnamon
1 tsp ground mixed spice
1 tsp bicarbonate of soda
250mls milk
115g black treacle
115g golden syrup
3 pieces stem ginger

8"/20cm deep round tin

cooking time:
50mins - 1hr @ 180°c

Method

In a small bowl, add the sugar, treacle, syrup and milk and heat in a microwave until dissolved and well combined, do not allow to boil. In a blender mix the flour, spices, soda and butter until finely blended and no trace of butter. Transfer the flour mix to a large mixing bowl and then add the sugar mix and stir well until it looks like a batter, then stir in the beaten egg. Now add the chopped stem ginger with a little of the ginger syrup for good measure. Pour into the lined cake tin and bake.

Sally's Top Tip - If you can bear to leave the cake for a day or two it will develop a sumptuous sticky top. A water icing made with some of the ginger syrup makes a nice topping if you fancy drizzling some over when the cake has cooled.

Lemon Drizzle Cake

Ingredients

115g soft margarine
170g s/r flour
285g caster sugar
1 tsp baking powder
1 lemon
2 eggs
4 tbsp milk

2lb/900g tin

cooking time:
50mins @ 180°c

Method

Cream the margarine and 170g of caster sugar, then mix in
the sifted flour, baking powder and beaten eggs, before finally
mixing in the grated lemon rind and milk to a smooth batter.
Put in a lined loaf tin and bake.

Mix the remaining 115g of caster sugar with the juice of the
lemon and once the cake is out of the oven, pierce it with
a skewer and pour over the lemon drizzle. Allow to cool
thoroughly before slicing.

Sally's Top Tip - It will keep in a cake tin for a
few days, if you can resist temptation for that long!

Chocolate Fudge Cake

Cake Ingredients

8"/20cm deep round tin

170g margarine
170g caster sugar
155g self raising flour
3 eggs
15g cocoa powder
1 tsp baking powder
1 tbsp hot water

cooking time:
40mins @ 180°c

Icing ingredients

50g butter
1 tbsp milk
1 tbsp golden syrup
15g cocoa
175g icing sugar

Method

Cream the margarine and the sugar, then mix in the sifted flour, baking powder & cocoa then add the beaten eggs and hot water(allow a boiled kettle to rest a while and use some of this water) then spoon into the lined cake tin.

When the cake has cooled make the icing as follows;
In a small bowl, gently melt the butter, milk and syrup in the microwave but do not allow it to get hot or the icing will look grainy and be rather difficult to spread on the cake.

Stir the butter mix and then add the sifted icing sugar and cocoa until a smooth glossy icing pulls away from the sides of the bowl. Apply liberally to the cake and allow to set before getting stuck in.

Moist Fruit Cake

Ingredients

8"/20cm deep round tin

115g margarine
225g dark brown sugar
225g self raising flour
2 eggs
500g bag of mixed dried fruit
284ml / 1/2pint cold water
200g glace cherries

cooking time:
1¼hrs @ 180°c

Method

Place the margarine, sugar, fruit, whole cherries and water into a medium saucepan and bring to the boil. Reduce the heat and simmer for 15mins. Take off the heat and allow to cool before adding the sifted flour and beaten eggs to the pan and mixing thoroughly. Finally spoon into the lined cake tin and bake.

Sally's Top Tip - Makes a fabulous alternative to Christmas Cake, and stays moist and lasts for several weeks, if given the chance.

Raspberry Bakewell Tart

Ingredients

100g butter
125g caster sugar
3 eggs
150g ground almonds
1 tsp almond extract
6 tbsp raspberry jam
375g pack chilled dessert
        shortcrust pastry
3 tbsp flaked almonds

23cm round flan tin
baking beans

cooking time:
25 - 30mins @ 190°c

Method

Roll out the pastry to line the greased flan tin, prick the pastry
with a fork and then chill in the fridge for 15mins before laying a
sheet of parchment paper on top and filling with baking beans.
Now bake for 15mins. Then remove the paper and beans and
return to the oven for a further 5-10 mins until the pastry is
golden brown in colour. Leave to one side until cool and then
spread the jam over, adding more as required.

Meanwhile use an electric whisk to beat together softened
butter and the sugar until pale and fluffy. Add the eggs one
by one and then the almond extract. With a spoon, fold in the
ground almonds and then pour over the jam, carefully spreading
around with a spatula to level off the top. Sprinkle on the flaked
almonds and then bake for 25 -30mins.

Sally's Top Tip - Ensure pastry is almost
cooked before adding the jam to prevent the "soggy
bottom" syndrome!

Apple & Sultana Oat Squares

Ingredients

225g butter
225g caster sugar
225g self raising flour
225g porridge oats
2 dessert apples
115g sultanas
2 tbsp runny honey
1 tsp bicarbonate of soda

9"/23cm square
cake tin

cooking time:
30 - 40mins @ 180°c

Method

In one large bowl, mix the oats, sifted flour and bicarbonate of soda. In another microwave bowl, place the butter, sugar and honey and carefully melt, mix thoroughly and ensure it is well blended but not too hot. Combine the two bowls together stirring well to combine all the ingredients and put to one side.

Peel, core and chop the apples into small chunks. Place half of the oats mix into the tin and level the top before adding the apples and sultanas, then cover with the remaining oat mix.

Cook until golden looking on the top, then leave to cool for at least 20mins before cutting into 9 – 12 portions.

Date & Walnut Loaf

Ingredients

115g butter or margarine
115g caster sugar
225g self raising flour
2 eggs
2-3 tsp ground mixed spice
6 tbsps milk
115g chopped walnuts
115g chopped dates

2 lb/900g loaf tin

cooking time:
1hr @ 180°c

Method

Cream the fat and the sugar, then mix in the sifted flour & spice. Add the milk at this point to loosen the mixture, then when it's all a smooth batter add the beaten eggs. Finally stir in the chopped dates & walnuts and spoon into the lined loaf tin.

Sally's Top Tip - Add a covering of Demerara sugar to the cake mix before putting in the oven for a lovely crunchy top.
Alternatively, when cooled top with a small amount of water icing and let it drip down the sides of the cake!

Carrot & Almond Cake

Ingredients

275g caster sugar
75g self raising flour
(or gluten free self raising flour)
5 eggs
240g ground almonds
480g grated carrot

8"/20cm round cake tin

cooking time:
1¼hrs @ 180°c

Topping ingredients

3 tbsp toasted flaked almonds
100g cream cheese
80g butter
80g icing sugar

Method

Separate the eggs and whisk the whites to soft peaks then put
to one side. In a large bowl whisk the egg yolks slowly adding
the caster sugar until thick and creamy. Stir in the grated carrot,
ground almonds and sifted flour to combine thoroughly.

Using a large metal spoon fold some of the egg white mix
into the carrot mixture then gently blend the remainder before
carefully spooning into the prepared cake tin and bake for 1 ¼
hours.

For the cream cheese topping, soften the butter and mix in the
sifted icing sugar, blend in the cream cheese, adding more icing
sugar if required to achieve a thick spreadable covering. Top
with the flaked almonds and leave until the icing has set.

Coffee & Walnut Sponge

Ingredients

225g butter or margarine
225g caster sugar
225g self raising flour
4 eggs
4 tbsp instant coffee
2 tbsp hot water
8-10 half walnuts
1 rounded tsp baking powder

2x 8"/20cm round
sandwich tins

cooking time:
25mins @ 180°c

Method

Cream the fat and the sugar, then mix in the sifted flour and the baking powder, then add the beaten eggs.

Mix the coffee granules in the hot water until dissolved, then add 1½tbsp of the coffee mix to the cake batter before pouring equal amounts into the greased and lined tins.

When the 2 sponges have cooled, make up some butter icing adding more of the coffee mix and sandwich the sponges together. Spreading a liberal amount of chopped walnuts on top of the butter icing is great. Position the half walnuts with a small amount of butter icing around the cake allowing one half per portion before finishing off with a dusting of icing sugar on top of the cake.

Sally's Top Tip - Soften the fat and sugar in the microwave to save on elbow grease! Spreading some butter icing on the underside of the top sponge will keep the chopped walnuts in place and stop the sponge from moving when cutting the cake.

Banana Choc Chip Cake

Ingredients

8"/20cm Deep round tin

170g margarine
170g granulated sugar
285g self raising flour
3 eggs
2tsp vanilla essence
2 – 3 ripe bananas
100g bag milk chocolate chips
½ tsp salt
½ tsp bicarbonate of soda

Cooking time:
1hr @ 170°C

Method

Cream the margarine and the sugar, and then mix in the sifted flour, salt and soda, and then the beaten eggs. In a separate bowl mash the bananas and add the vanilla essence and the choc chips, testing just one or two to ensure they're ok :)

Add the banana mix to the cake mix and stir well for even distribution then spoon into the lined tin.

Sally's Top Tip - This cake will last well in a tin. It freezes really well and is an excellent way to use up those bruised bananas that come home in packed lunch boxes!

Cappuccino Tray Bake

Ingredients

225g butter or margarine
225g caster sugar
225g self raising flour
4 eggs
1 tsp baking powder
1 tbsp hot water
1 tbsp cocoa powder
2 tbsp coffee granules

9"x12"/23x30cm
tray bake tin

cooking time:
40mins @ 180°c

Icing Ingredients

57g butter
170g icing sugar
115g white chocolate
3 tbsp milk

Method

Mix together the coffee granules, cocoa powder and 2 tbsps of very hot water. Cream the fat and the sugar, then mix in the sifted flour, baking powder, then add the beaten eggs.

Finally stir through the coffee liquid ensuring everything is combined before pouring the mix into the prepared tin. Bake until risen and springy to touch.

When the sponge has cooled, remove from the tin and make up the butter icing as follows; gently melt the chocolate, butter and milk, stirring to combine before adding the sifted icing sugar. Spread over the top of the cake and finish off with a dusting of cocoa powder on top of the cake.

Apple & Cinnamon Loaf

Ingredients

150g butter or margarine
150g caster sugar
200g self raising flour
2 eggs
2-3 tsp ground mixed spice
3 tbsps milk
200g sultanas
1 or 2 apples peeled, cored
and chopped
Demerara sugar (to sprinkle)

2 lb/900g loaf tin

cooking time:
1hr – 1hr 10mins @ 180°c

Method

Cream the fat and the sugar, then mix in the sifted flour & spice.
Add the milk at this point to loosen the mixture, then when it's all
a smooth batter add the beaten eggs. Finally stir in the chopped
apple and the sultanas, then spoon into the lined loaf tin. Add
a covering of Demerara sugar to the cake mix before putting in
the oven for a lovely crunchy top.

Sally's Top Tip - Soak the sultanas in a bowl
with a tea bag and some boiling water to make them more
juicy and swollen before you begin making the cake, then
drain the water (and remove the tea bag!!!) before adding
to the cake mix.

Blueberry & Almond Cake

Ingredients

200g butter or margarine
200g caster sugar
125g self raising flour
(or gluten free self raising flour)
4 eggs
125g ground almonds
150g blueberries
1tsp almond extract

8"/20cm round cake tin

cooking time:
1hr @ 180°c

Method

Rinse the blueberries and leave to dry on a sheet of kitchen towel. Separate the eggs and whisk the whites to soft peaks then put to one side.

Cream together the fat and 175g of the sugar until pale and fluffy, then add the egg yolks and almond extract.

Sift all but 1tsp of the flour into the bowl and stir gently to combine thoroughly. Shake the blueberries in the tsp of flour until evenly coated, than put to one side

Whisk in the remaining 25g of sugar into the egg whites and then fold in the ground almonds.

Using a large metal spoon fold some of the egg white mix into the creamed mixture then gently blend the remainder before carefully spooning into the prepared cake tin.

Scatter the floured blueberries on the top of the mixture before placing in the oven.

Whole Orange Cake

Ingredients

8"/20cm round cake tin

50g butter or margarine, melted
140g caster sugar
85g self raising flour
3 eggs
100g ground almonds
1 orange

cooking time:
40 - 45mins @ 180°c

Icing Ingredients

85g icing sugar
1 orange

Method

Put one of the oranges in a small saucepan, cover with cold water, bring the boil then cover and simmer for 1 hr. Remove and cool. Chop, remove the pips then whizz, rind and all, in a small processor until smooth.

Whisk the sugar and eggs together until pale and fluffy, then sift the flour and ground almonds into the bowl and using a large metal spoon fold gently. Then add in the orange puree and the melted butter before carefully spooning into the prepared cake tin.

Bake for 40-45mins then allow to cool before icing. Juice the remaining orange and mix with the icing sugar then drizzle over the top of the cake.

Sally's Top Tip - Chocolate fudge icing from the Chocolate cake recipe can also be spread over the cooled cake to make a sticky Chocolate Orange cake.

Date Slice

Ingredients

75g butter
75g dark brown sugar
75g plain flour
100g porridge oats
250g stoned dates
100ml water

7"/18cm square cake tin

cooking time:
15 - 20mins @ 180°c

Method

Chop the dates and cook in a pan with the water and 25g of the sugar until soft and like a paste but not sloppy.

In a blender mix together the flour and butter and remaining sugar then transfer to a large bowl before stirring in the oats.

Put half of the mix into the tin and level firmly, then add the date paste, now top with the remaining oat mix patting down gently. Cook until golden. Cut into approx. 9 portions while still hot then leave to cool in the tin.

Chocolate Cornflake Cakes

Ingredients

57g butter or margarine
57g icing sugar
85g cornflakes
85g sultanas
2 tbsp golden syrup
3 tbsp cocoa powder

Method

Melt the butter or margarine and syrup gently in the microwave, then mix in the sifted icing sugar and cocoa powder. Add the cornflakes and sultanas until everything is coated in the chocolate mix.

Arrange the cupcake cases on a tray and fill with spoonful of the mix to the size required.

Leave to cool before enjoying, they'll keep for a while in a tin if not eaten before! They can freeze but are at their best when fresh.

Sally's Top Tip - Top with Mini Eggs for Easter cakes, Smarties, other sweets or soft fruit of your choice for other special occasions. Other breakfast cereals work really well too, so be as imaginative as you like, Fruit & Fibre, Rice Krispies, Sultana Bran, etc.

Victoria Sponge

Ingredients

225g butter or margarine
225g caster sugar
225g self raising flour
4 eggs
1 tbsp hot water
1 rounded tsp baking powder
jam of choice

2x 8"/20cm round
sandwich tins

cooking time:
25mins @ 180°c

Method

Cream the fat and the sugar, then mix in the sifted flour and baking powder, then add the beaten eggs.

Finally stir through the hot water before pouring equal amounts into the greased and lined tins and bake.

When the 2 sponges have cooled, make up some butter icing and sandwich the sponges together. Spreading a liberal amount of either strawberry, raspberry, blackcurrant jam or even lemon curd over the butter icing before putting the top sponge on can make for a more colourful cake. Finish off with a dusting of icing sugar on top of the cake.

Sally's Top Tip - Soften the fat and sugar in the microwave to save on elbow grease! Adding fresh fruit is a beautiful finishing touch but ensure the cake is eaten the same day or the cake can go soggy.......heaven forbid!!

Lime & Coconut Drizzle Loaf

Cake Ingredients

100g butter or margarine
175g caster sugar
175g self raising flour
2 eggs
½ 400g can coconut milk
2 limes

Icing Ingredients

1 lime
½ 400g can coconut milk
200g caster sugar

2 lb/900g loaf tin

cooking time:
40mins @ 180°c

Method

Cream the fat and the sugar, then mix in the sifted flour.
When it's all a smooth batter, add ½ of the can of coconut
milk then the beaten eggs and the grated zest of 2 limes. Pour
into the loaf tin and bake for 40mins until golden and a skewer
comes out clean.

Meanwhile make the icing by boiling together the remaining
coconut milk and 150g of the caster sugar for 5 mins until quite
thick and syrupy. Stir in the juice of 2 limes and leave to cool.

Mix the remaining caster sugar with the finely grated zest of the
3rd lime until you have a sticky damp green paste.

When the loaf is cooked pour over a little of the icing, waiting for
it to be absorbed before adding more. Leave to cool thoroughly
and remove from the tin, adding the lime sugar sprinkles on top.

Pineapple Upside Down Sponge

Ingredients

225g butter or margarine
225g caster sugar
225g self raising flour
4 eggs
1 tsp baking powder
1 tbsp hot water
1 tin of 8 pineapple slices
8 glace cherries, halved

9"x12"/23x30cm
tray bake tin

cooking time:
40mins @ 180°c

Method

Cut the pineapple slices in half and arrange on the bottom of
the lined tin, then place one half of a cherry into the round
space of the pineapple, cut side up.

Cream the fat and the sugar, then mix in the sifted flour, baking
powder, then add the beaten eggs. Finally stir through the hot
water before carefully pouring over the pineapple and cherries.

Bake for 40mins and then invert onto a cooling rack. When cold,
cut into the 16 portions and eat cold as a cake or heat up with
some custard for an old fashioned pudding.

Sally's Top Tip - Cut and wash the glace
cherries to remove the syrup before putting in the tin.
Small dried apricots or walnut halves or pecans could be
used if glace cherries are not your favourite!

Keswick Mountain Rescue

Keswick Mountain Rescue Team was formed after the particularly long and arduous rescue on the Shark's Fin of Great Gable in 1946. In those days any rescues were carried out by local farmers or others who happened to be in the area. There was little in the way of equipment and, if the casualty could not make their own way off, the only form of stretcher was often a gate. In 1947 Colonel "Rusty" Westmorland thought that the time had come to form an organised mountain rescue team so he put an advertisement in the "Keswick Reminder" asking for volunteers to come forward. From there Keswick had one of the first mountain rescue teams in the country. We pride ourselves that we have always been at the forefront of developments in all things mountain rescue, both on the fell and behind the scenes.

Keswick Mountain Rescue Team now has about 45 volunteer members from many different walks of life, who turn out at a moment's notice, at all hours of the day and night, 7 days a week, everyday of the year to assist people who have got into difficulty on the fells. We do much more than rescue people on the mountains, most team members are qualified Swift Water Rescue Technicians who work in rivers and flood situations, some are RYA trained boat handlers (we are the primary response for rescues on Derwent Water), some members also have trained search dogs. Whilst we are Keswick based, and the hills around Keswick are our patch, we are available to attend incidents throughout Cumbria and even beyond. As you can imagine we also have to do a lot of training to keep skills to a high standard in subjects as diverse as First Aid, technical rope rescue, winter skills, on and off-road driving, working with Coastguard and air ambulance helicopters and much more. This, along with all the behind the scenes activity - admin, vehicle maintenance etc does not come cheaply so we are really grateful to all the people who so generously support us, often in innovative and personal ways.

Sally's cakes are a prime example of this and we really appreciate the results that her and Keith's efforts have achieved on behalf of Glencoe Guest House – and yours for buying the cakes and this book. Enjoy both.

Andy Jones
Keswick Mountain Rescue

Notes

....
....
....
....
....
....
....
....
....
....
....
....
....
....
....
....
....
....
....
....

We would like to thank the following Keswick businesses for selling these books and giving 100% of the profits to the Keswick Mountain Rescue Team.